T0142584

BABYSITTER 1

BABYSITTER 1

Annie Lee

To order additional copies of this book, contact:
Xlibris
1-888-795-4274
www.Xlibris.com
Orders@Xlibris.com
726562

CONTENTS

DEDICATION

I dedicate this book to my mother,(my namesake), Annie McCoy Petty, who went home to be with the Lord, January 7, 2014. My late step father James Green Sr., grandfather, and grandmother, (Adam and Corine Mack McCoy) my deceased sisters, and brother, Cora Bell Cannon, Lela Walker, Evelyn McCoy, Steven Lynn McCoy, my (uncle), Adam McCoy Jr., my lovely (niece,) Deandra McCoy, and my oldest brother in law who is deceased, Lester G. Cannon.

ACKNOWLEDGMENTS

I thank God for giving me this title to this book. I thank my husband, Johnnie Hackett Jr. I thank God for my children, Twana, Christopher, Natalie, because they taught me how to pray and to stand on the Word of God. I thank God for my family, because they taught me how to witness. I thank God for my enemies because they have taught me how to be blessed. I want to acknowledge the "Mighty Women of God Five O'clock A.M. Prayer Line" for more than twenty-five years of praying for me and my family. Prayer has allowed me to be revived, restored, renewed, strengthened and be refreshed in the Word of God. Prayer also delivers, heal and set us free from all types of demonic activity that would bind us from receiving the best from GOD.

I thank God for the Pastors and Leaders that I've had in the Ministry that have taught me the Good News about the Bible. I also thank God for the men, women, boys, and girls that have encouraged me when I was discouraged.

I'm grateful for the Christians and testimonies that I have heard all around the world on National Television, TBN, Revivals, and through Church Conferences. I don't want to leave any one out because; the people in this world are in my prayers daily.

Thank you, Thank you and Thank you!

FOREWORD

First, I would like to give praise and honor to my Lord and Savior Jesus Christ for his mercy and grace. I will give honor to Minister Annie Lee for her faith and commitment to write this book and fulfill her destiny.

This book will instruct you to make Jesus your Lord and Savior. It is God desire that we grow and mature in the things of God. He does not want you to remain baby Christians. In this this book there are scriptures and prayers given by divine revelation so that you will no longer be just a hearer of the word, but a doer of God's word. This book is filled with the truth of God's word. Once you embrace these truths, you will no longer be on milk. You will be able to understand and digest the strong meat of His word. You can prosper and move to your destiny and purpose in life.

Minister Jannet Martin
Founder of Command your Morning Prayer Line Ministry
Humble Texas

First, I reverence our Almighty for giving Minister Annie Lee a heart and passion to help people in need and a special love to see people set free in Christ. I have known Min. Lee over 15 years and observed her love for God. It has grown and is growing each year. She has been found faithful in the Lord, prayer, her family and ministry. This book "Babysitter 1" will help people to identify themselves, acknowledge or accept Christ. Then start building a relationship to maintain mental and spiritual freedom. This is a powerful tool and guide that would help you get out of bondage mentally and spiritually. Min. Lee is excellent in explaining chapter by chapter Freedom is Available, Obtainable and Sustainable through our Lord and Savior Jesus Christ.

This is a must read!!!!!

Minister Veronica Carouthers
Holy Ghost Heavy Hitters

I would like to congratulate Mrs. Annie Lee for a job well done writing this book. It is very inspirational to everyone who gets this book and read it. Not only to those who are locked up in prison, but those who are in prison in their own mind. Please accept God in your life and allow him to become the center of your joy. Your life situation can turn around for the better, if you give your life totally and completely over to God. You will no longer have to be locked up behind jail or prison bars because, you will know how to submit to God. You can be free to witness to your brothers and sisters to come to know the God you serve. Jehovah Jireh will come into your life, who is God your provider. You can be victorious in God. Please allow God to Change and rearrange some things in your life. Romans 8:28

Bishop Clayton W. Powell
Deliverance Church

Hold your head up

Hold your head up high.

The Lord is mighty in battle,

And he is drawing nigh.

If you've ever

used drugs and alcohol,

or been in the Correctional Facilities too!

Open your mouth and ask the Lord;

What must I do?

He'll tell you to hold your head up,

Hold your head up high!

Because the Lord is mighty in battle

And he is drawing nigh.

Chapter One

SATAN WANTS TO CONTROL
YOUR LIFE

The reason the enemy wants you to act like a baby or small child is so that he can control your life. In Texas Department of Corrections there are many guards to prevent you from harming others and yourself. There have been fights in the chow room, bathrooms, jail cells, or outside during recreation or exercise activities. You have to be watched so that you and other inmates will not get into any trouble. You are watched like a baby. The premises have cameras to monitor all movement and activities inside and outside of the facility at all times. The Jailers monitor you and the other inmates to see if there are any unlawful actions going on that are prohibited in the Facility.

Some parents have monitors on their babies. They want to make sure that the babies or children are not in any danger and that everything is okay while they are sleeping.

When a small child is in the home, cautions are taken because there are hazardous chemicals that are under cabinets, or in the home that you do not want the babies to eat or drink that'll make them sick or kill them.

There are men and women that like to experiment with consuming chemicals, drugs, embalming fluid, crack, paint thinner, prescription drugs, alcohol with pills and many other chemicals that our mind and body do not agree with.

We need to continue to pray for those addictive ways that we have allowed to attach themselves to us. If you stand before God and talk to him; He will answer you. Go to a place where there is quietness and wait to hear from God. In the book of **(1 Kings 19:12)** God gave revelation to Elijah; **"And after the earthquake a fire; but the Lord was not in the fire: and after the fire a still small voice."** God will speak to us in a small voice or a whisper. We must train our spirits to hear the voice of God. We can spend time in his word and prayer daily, that's when we develop a relationship with God.

We sometimes don't want to obey the words of the Bible or do things the right way, that's why God said that flesh is an enmity to Him. Flesh wants to do things the wrong way and stay in trouble with God. Why? There is pleasure in sin and there's pleasure in righteousness. When we continue to do what is wrong we change the truth of God to a lie and the enemy will have us believing that we are living the right way. Some people do not want their lives to be controlled by God or anyone; they love wickedness and the power of darkness in their lives.

In the book of **(Romans 1:18-32)**

[18] For the wrath of God is revealed from heaven against all ungodliness and unrighteousness of men, who hold the truth in unrighteousness;

[32] Who knowing the judgment of God, that they which commit such things are worthy of death, not only do the same, but have pleasure in them that do them.

(Romans 8:8) So then they that are in the flesh cannot please God. If you want to live right, walk right, talk right, you must be led by God's spirit. Communicating with God will keep us from getting into a lot of unnecessary trouble. **(Hebrew 13:16) But to do good and to communicate forget not: for with such sacrifices God is well pleased.**

When you are released from Jail or Correctional Facilities you should know how you should conduct yourself in everyday life. You must be careful not to fall in the entrapments that have ensnared you before. There's an old saying, that you can't teach an old dog new tricks.

If you have an open mind to the things of God and what he wants to do in your life, you will make a change. You will have an open mind to do better and be better. You do not want to be watched or monitored for the rest of your life. You don't need anyone to babysit you twenty-four hours a day, seven days a week. Only babies need that type of care and to be watched and looked after all day long. Grown men and women should know how to conduct themselves. God wants us to be free to serve him not Satan.

For God so loved the world that he gave his only begotten Son, that whosoever believeth in him should not perish, but have everlasting life. (John 3:16) God loves us all and He is no respecter of persons: He allowed his only Son to die for our sins and we know that we have a right to the tree of life and go to Heaven when we leave here. We have a right to the blessings of God. We also need to do right and live right toward God.

Time out!! You want others to do what you say but you don't want to do what God wants you to do. Many times I wanted my children to obey me and the things that I said.

I didn't obey God's word and the things he said. We know that it's wrong and we need to ask God for forgiveness so that we can move on in God. We <u>must</u> be doers of the word and not hearers only. **(James 1:22) But be ye doers of the word, and not hearers only, deceiving your own selves.** There comes a time in life that we must be trustworthy to ourselves and our families. As long as we are living in this world it is never too late to turn our lives around.

We sing this hymn in Church: As the song says Reach out and touch somebody's hand and make this world a better place if you can. I substitute if for cause, because I know each individual can change and, lives around them would change too. So I sing it like this, Reach out and touch somebody's hand, make this world a better place because you can. (Try singing it this way sometime.)

(1 Corinthians 15:33) Be not deceived: Evil communications corrupt good manners. Two or more babies or children can be playing or sitting together and if one has picked up a bad habit or says something that is not okay. The others will eventually say or do the same thing. Babies don't understand everything because

they are learning about life every day. We have been taught right from wrong.

We should press toward the mark of the higher calling in Christ Jesus. (Philippians 3:14) Strive every day to do better and be better. Don't let anyone control your spirit but GOD. You are not a baby, you are an overcomer. You are also a mature man or woman in Christ Jesus, Amen!

In the book **of (II Corinthians 13:1)** If you are sincere about seeking God, **he will come in the mouth of two or three witnesses shall every word be established.** Two or three people will tell you some of the similar quotations that have to do with the same subject about something pertaining to you. They will not know that another person told you the same similar quotation or phrase unless you explain to them that you've heard this before. It may be within a day, a week, a month, or years. Then, you will be saying this is the second or third time that I have heard this saying to me. The Lord wants to get your attention to be obedient to do things his way. I've known men and women who got saved and came out of prison or jail and prospered. They changed their mindset about the way to conquer life to the fullest. In the midst of their perseverance God prospered them. **(Psalms 35:27) says Let them shout for joy, and be glad, that favour my righteous cause: yea, let them say continually, <u>Let the Lord be magnified, which hath pleasure in the prosperity of his servant.</u>**

There are some things that you do in life that you know it's not right according to the will of God. Understand that you are acting like a child or a baby that don't know wrong from right. Evil is for real and you will find out how serious it is, if you have ever had a stronghold in your life. It is something that you want to be delivered from. Relationships, companionships, friendships, over eating, drugs, cigarettes, alcoholism, gambling, homosexuality, lesbian, sex addicts, controlling, and lying, these are only a few of the strongholds. When you decide that I'm going to be the man or woman that God wants you to be, you have acknowledged there is a stronghold in your life. You will want a change in your life. You may not have a multitude of friends, but God is a friend that sticks closer than a brother. **(Proverbs 18:24) A man that hath friends must shew himself friendly, and there is a friend that**

sticketh closer than a brother. God's son Jesus can be your friend today. You must give your time, money in some situations, and allow him to be a friend to you, and most of all trust God to meet your needs.

My motto is: **Pray to stay, fast to last, give to live.**

(Proverbs 17:17a) A friend loveth at all times, and a brother is born for adversity. I love my sisters, brothers, and the family, but I have a friend that will tell me what the word of God says.

When my family and I don't see eye to eye on some situations in life, they will try to comfort me in their own way. It is the word of God that I need to set me free. **(John 8:32) And ye shall know the truth and the truth will make you free.** When you discover the truth in Jesus Christ it sets you free emotionally, oppression ally, psychologically, and spiritually. Religion will confuse a person; God's truth brings about freedom, wholeness and positive growth. Receiving the truth in your heart will transform the human personality and causes a change in a person's behavior. This is because people can only know truth by practicing it.

(Proverbs 18:1-2) {Student Bible} A man who isolates himself seeks his own desire. He rages against all judgment. A fool has no delight in understanding, But in expressing his own heart. {KJV}Through desire a man having separated himself, seeketh and intermeddleth with all wisdom. The enemy is Satan, and he don't want you to get your praise on in Church, or hear any powerful testimonies so that you can be an over comer. You can have victory in any situation because **God can turn a curse into a blessing. (Nehemiah 13:2b)**

In life you don't have to continue doing the things you used to do because you are not a baby. Grow up so that when Jesus comes back you can go up and be with the Lord.

Take into consideration what the Lord require of us, and that is to do good, justly and be fair to our neighbors, family, friends, and our enemies no matter what's going on in life.

✓ Pray this prayer and every prayer with a sincere heart and mind that you want God to help you defeat the enemy from defeating you and controlling your life.

Prayer

Father God in the name of Jesus, help me to meditate in the Bible and become mature. **(Psalms 1:2)** Help me to meditate upon your Word day and night so that whatsoever I do, I may prosper. I will not need anyone to watch over me as a baby needs a babysitter, to watch him or her so they won't do any harm to themselves or anybody. Satan will not control my life or my mind, because I have the mind of Christ. **(II Timothy 1:7) For God hath not given us the spirit of fear; but of power, and of love, and of a sound mind.)** Lord, I thank you for teaching me to have the mind of Christ in making decisions in my everyday life. I trust you for helping me be the best that I can be. Satan will not control my life and I will be more than a conqueror. I have the victory! **In Jesus' name, Amen!**

Chapter Two

YOU MUST HAVE A MADE UP MIND

There is a song that says; that my mind is made up, and I'm on my way up, going on with the LORD. You must have a made up mind that you don't have to be watched all the time. When you're incarcerated, pray to God to help you get yourself together and not be incarcerated again unless God has a purpose for you to go behind bars to minister to others.

You have to get so close to God and tell him like Jacob did: **(Genesis 32:26) I'm not going to turn you a loose until you bless me.** Continue talking to God and letting him know that you will not turn him a loose until he blesses you. You let God know that you want to be close to him and to be used by him and he will bless your wants, your needs and your desires. **(Psalms 23:1) (Philippians 4:19) (Psalms 37:4)** Jacob continued serving God in Chapter 35. He told his people to put away the strange gods that were among them, and be clean, and change your garments. **(Genesis 35:3)** He wanted to make an altar to GOD because God answered him when he was in distress. Jacob brother wanted to kill him. Jacob testified to his people because he had known GOD. You got to have a made up mind because you can't deliver what God has not delivered. You can't make any person in this world act right or love you the way you want to be loved. That's false and fake love. Pray for them and ask God to let his will be done in their lives, toward you and others. Therefore if God don't deliver them out of bondage, you can't do it.

Keep the faith in God and he will change them when the time is right. Also he will give them and you powerful testimonies.

(Exodus 34:14) For thou shalt worship no other god: for the Lord, whose name is Jealous, is a jealous God. God wants to be in control, not us, because flesh will mess up things in our life. We need to ask God about every situation in our life. I thank God that we all need him because He knows how to fix every situation. **(Genesis 18:14) Is there anything too hard for the Lord?**

I know that you have seen someone in your family serving God that were blessed, and have been a blessing to someone. They may have strayed from the Word one time or another. They got back on track and started reading the Bible and praying.

In **(Psalms 73:17)** David saw the wicked prospering in the world. He thought that only the wicked would prosper.

Verse seventeen says that when he went in the sanctuary of God, then he understood the wicked people's end. **(Psalms 73:22-28)** David desired none upon earth except God because he knew God was the strength of his heart. **Verse twenty-eight** says, but it is good for me to draw near to God: I have put my trust in the Lord God, that I may declare all thy works. When you draw near to God you will have peace, protection, salvation, deliverance, healing, prosperity and the Holy Spirit will be your guide.

Abraham, **(Exodus 18:19)** Job, **(Job 42:2)** Deborah, **(Judges 4:9)** Apostles, **(Acts 5:19)** Esther, **(Esther 4:16)** Jonah, **(Jonah 2:9)** and many other people in the Old and New Testament had a made up mind about God and acknowledge who he was.

When you realize that you can do nothing on your own you will need God's help. Faith steps in and move mountains for you.

When you know how good God has been to you, your family, and friends, you will keep a made up mind about serving God and allowing him to continue using you. When you keep thanking God, he will give you favour because you love him. He will make you the head and not the tail, above and not beneath.

You can't let anyone or anything persuade you to do wrong. Trouble is easy to get into but, hard to get out of it. I look at professional business entrepreneurs' lives and realized with all the money that they have made in their business, they had to have a made up mind to prosper and sometimes many of them thank God for wisdom to prosper. I know many of them had encouragers to help them succeed and persevere.

The Word of the Lord tells us that we can't have two masters. Will you continue to serve GOD or Satan? **(Matthew 6:24) No man can serve two masters; for either he will hate one and love the other; or else he will hold to the one, and despise the other. Ye cannot serve God and mammon.**

When your mind is made up to serve the Lord with all your heart, you have fallen in love with the Lord Jesus. You will want to walk uprightly before him. **(Psalms 84:11-12)** says; **For the Lord is a sun and shield: the lord will give grace and glory: no good thing will he withhold from them that walk uprightly. (12) O Lord of host, blessed is the man that trusteth in thee.** Talking to God and thanking him always for the good and bad will keep Gods favour on your life. Minister to him like he ministers to us. Letting him know that if it had not been him on your side that you don't know where you would be.

In the book of **(Ecclesiastes 8:11) Because sentence against an evil work is not executed speedily, therefore the heart of the sons of men is fully set in them to do evil. Though a sinner do evil an hundred times and his days be prolonged, yet surely I know that it shall be well with them that fear God, which fear before him: But it shall not be well with the wicked, neither shall he prolong his days, which are as a shadow; because he feareth not before God.** Because God doesn't chastise us instantly when we do wrong and wicked, it does not mean that he is pleased with our wrong doing. **(Malachi 3:13-18) Your words have been stout against me, saith the Lord. Yet ye say, what have we spoken against thee?** Verse 14 says: **Ye have said, It is vain to serve God: and what profit is it that we have kept his ordinance, and that we have walked mournfully before the Lord of hosts.** Verse 15: **and know we call the proud Happy; yea, they that work wickedness are set up; yea, they that tempt God are even delivered.**

(James1:8) A double-minded man is unstable in all his ways. (James 4:8) Draw nigh to God and he will draw nigh to you. Cleanse your hands, ye sinners; and purify your hearts, ye double-minded.

A man's or a woman's choice determines their destiny. I know that we are not perfect and we sometimes allow the wrong people or things into our lives. When you can come to yourself and know that you have made the wrong choice. Ask God for forgiveness and know that he is a rewarder of them that diligently seek him. (Hebrew 11:6) Trusting God to restore you and not to ever give up no matter what you've done.

"Wash you, make you clean; put away the evil of your doings from before mine eyes; cease to do evil; Learn to do well; seek judgment, relieve the oppressed, judge the fatherless, plead for the widow." (Isaiah 1:16-17 KJV) There comes a time in life that you must trust God when you get tired of trying to make certain things happen. (Do you know that witchcraft or control is not the way God wanted it?) Read the Word and talk to the Master of the universe; who is God. He is a mystery, but he has power that you will never comprehend or know how much he can do.

Please pray with a sincere heart and mind wanting God to fix everything that is in your life that needs to be fixed. Your mind has to be made up and you have to count the cost. There are so many Christians being killed (put to sleep) today because they Know God.

In the book of **Acts 7:1-53** It is called Stephen's Address: He spoke of Abraham, Joseph, Moses, Joshua, David and Solomon. These men were servants of God truly trusted in the Lord. They allowed the Holy Spirit's presence to bless them. Verse 51 says; You stiffed-necked and uncircumcised in heart and ears! You always resist the Holy Spirit; as your fathers did, so do you.

Acts 7:54-60 After Stephen shared his belief because his mind was made up to live is Christ and to die is gain. Verse 55 says that he was full of the Holy Spirit and looked up in Heaven and seen the glory of God, and Jesus standing on the right hand of God. They took Stephen out of the city and stoned him and he called on Jesus to receive his spirit. He knelt down and then cried out this time with a loud voice. Do not charge them for this sin. He did not want them to be charged with murder. When Stephen asked for forgiveness, he fell asleep. We call it dead or died and God call it fell asleep.

You can't be doubleminded about serving God or being his disciples.

I will let you know now that you will be tested by the enemy to see if your mind is really made up!!

Prayer

Father, I come before you today to ask you to forgive me for all my sins. I thank you hearing my prayer and listening to me. I don't want to be double –minded about my Christian walk with you. I will put my trust totally in you and be blessed. I'm also asking you to bless my mind, my thoughts and the decisions that I make and those that I have to make in the future. Let my desires line up with your will for my life. Lord, I'm praying not only for me but for my family, friends, neighbors and enemies that we all have a made up mind towards you. We will walk right, talk right, live right, and pray right. I also believe and trust you that my family, friends, enemies will be saved and come to repentance. I pray for no distractions to hinder this prayer. In Jesus' name, Amen

Chapter Three

YOU CAN'T HAVE FEAR AND WALK IN VICTORY!

When you want victory in your life and for others also, fear is not an option. I've heard people say; I don't want a lot of blessings from God because someone that I know or love dearly will be mad at me. We should not have fear about the blessings or prosperity that God gives you. If you have sown seeds in the Kingdom of God, helped the poor, widows and widowers; the Lord will bless you bountifully. This is not being boastful or bragging but, this is a testimony. **(Psalms 35:27) Let them shout for joy, and be glad that favour my righteous cause; yea, let them say continually, let the Lord be magnified, which hath pleasure in the prosperity of his servant.** I want everything that God wants me to have. It's time to shout and be happy, because God is righteous and he knows what he's doing in our life. The Lord is greater than we could ever imagine and he wants us to be blessed. **(Psalms 23:1) The Lord is my shepherd and shall not want.** Everything that you want God's got it and if he doesn't give it to you now, you will know the reason later on in life. **(Psalms 37:4) Delight thyself also in the Lord; and he shall give thee the desires of thine heart.** You will have to spend time in Church, (Ministers and fellowship with other believers) in the Word of God, (reading and meditating in his Word) and through testimonials, (TV, revivals, conferences, prayer and fasting).

He will bless you, and you will love to bless others. **(Philippians 4:19) But my God shall supply all your need according to his riches**

in glory by Christ Jesus. He knows all your needs and because he's God it is just a need to him. He is so powerful that the need could be a thousand things that you need and he works in mysterious ways. He will supply the need for your good. **(Romans 8:28) And we know that all things work together for good to them that love God, to them who are called according to His purpose.** When we want, desire and need are according to God's purpose, you will have joy and great pleasure in receiving it.

You are in a contest to win. There are evil forces against good forces. There is a war going on and it's up to you to triumph over the power of darkness with the help of God. **(Ephesians 6:10-18) says; Finally my brethren, be strong in the Lord, and in the power of his might. Put on the whole armour of God that ye may be able to stand against the wiles of the devil. For we wrestle not against flesh and blood, but against principalities, against powers, against rulers of the darkness of this world, against spiritual wickedness in high places. Wherefore take unto you the whole armour of God that ye may be able to withstand in the evil day, and having all, to stand.** Men and women of God must stay close to God and believe every word he says in the BIBLE. Why? Every scripture in the Bible is true. I came from a family of thirteen sisters and brothers. The Bible scriptures that I have quoted have changed my family that they know something about God. We are not what we should be, but we are not what we use to be. I continue standing as an intercessor for them. **Verse 14 says; Stand therefore, having your loins girt about with the truth, and having on the breastplate of righteousness; (15) and your feet shod with the preparation of the gospel of peace.** You got to know the truth of the Word of God and ask the Holy Spirit to help you. The Spirit of God that he sent to help us in the time of need. You got to have a will or desire to do things God way or no way at all. Darkness does not want you to do what is right. Evil loves things done the wrong way. You will have to walk in peace and not strife. I'm always asking God to forgive me of all my sins every day. I might of thought or said something wrong that was not of God. **(16) Above all, taking the shield of faith, wherewith ye shall be able to quench all the fiery darts of the wicked. (17) And the helmet of salvation, and the sword of the Spirit, which is the word of God.** You got to fight darkness with faith in God. We have everything we need because he told us to put on the whole armor of God so that we can triumph and have joy, victory, and success in this life. **Verse 18 says; Praying always with all prayer and supplication in the Spirit, and watching thereunto with all perseverance and supplication for all saints;** When you pray be sincere about what you are praying about because God knows your heart. Don't give up on God and he will not give up on you. Don't stop praying and thanking him for the VICTORY.

- **(II Timothy 1:7) For God hath not given us the spirit of fear; but of power, and of love, and of a sound mind.** Again I'm giving you this scripture because God wants you to memorize it. This fear is from Satan if you are walking in darkness. If you know God, you will have power, love, and you know that nothing can keep you from getting yourself together and being the man or woman that God wants you to be.

In the book of Joshua; when you would have good success. (**Joshua 1:8, 9**) when you study God's word and meditate upon it day and night, he promised that:

⁸ This book of the law shall not depart out of thy mouth; but thou shalt meditate therein day and night, that thou mayest observe to do according to all that is written therein: for then thou shalt make thy way prosperous, and then thou shalt have good success. Verse 9 says; Have not I commanded thee? Be strong and of good courage; be not afraid, neither be thou dismayed: for the Lord thy God is with thee withersoever thou goest.

- Fear will keep you from the promises of God. You will be fearful to walk in the destiny of what God has called you to be and to do. You must be strong in the Lord and have good courage.
- The only fear that you must be walking in is the fear of the Lord. And then the comfort of His Holy Spirit will bless you and strengthen you.

Proverbs 29:25 says: **The fear of man brings a snare. But whosoever trusts in the Lord shall be safe.**

Isaiah 35:4 says: Say to those who are fearful – hearted,
Be strong, do not fear! Behold your God will come with vengeance,
With the recompense (payback) of God; He will come and save you.

Prayer

Father God, in the name of Jesus, we come to you to ask for forgiveness for all of our sins that we may obtain grace and mercy in this time of prayer. I bind the spirit of fear that wants to stop me from moving forward and I loose an excellent spirit upon me as in the book of (Daniel 6:3) Then this Daniel was preferred above the presidents and princes, because an excellent spirit was in him; and the king thought to set him over the whole realm. Lord, I also pray that me, my family, friends, and enemies, prosper like Daniel did in Daniel 6:28. Lord, I thank you for favor upon me and my family's lives. Lord if I have forgotten to pray about anything, I'm asking you to fix it right now for me in Jesus name. Amen!

Chapter Four

THE LORD LOOSETH
THE PRISONERS

In the book of **(Psalms 146:7)**, at the end of the seventh verse: **The Lord looseth the prisoners**. There are many women and men and children that have been and some still are in prison. **Chapter 146** is telling all those that are incarcerated facilities that they need a Savior. They need someone that they can confide in and trust. The Bible tells you that you cannot trust leaders, because leaders are human beings also. You need God on your side to fix whatever is broken in your life. Ask God to forgive you of all your sins and talk to him as though he's right there in front of you and you don't have to speak out loud. God knows what you are going to ask him before you speak. He wants to communicate with you. If you are going to be strong in life you are going to have to trust God. He's allowed you to be on earth for a purpose. He can use you in prison to be his mouthpiece and speak to his people.

You must be filled with his Holy Spirit so that you can grow in truth. Some people claim that they have been filled with God's Holy Spirit and don't have any fruit in their lives. Once you have been saved and filled with God's spirit you will have to keep feeding it with the Word of God and prayer. They want to use God's people or get over on them by taking some type of property that they own, self-confidence from them or defaming their character. The Lord sees everything that's going on in your life. **(Galatians 6:7) Be not deceived; God is not mocked; for whatsoever a man soweth, that shall he also reap.**

(Verse 8) For he that soweth to his flesh shall of the flesh reap corruption; but he that soweth to the Spirit shall of the Spirit reap life everlasting. Whoever does wrong to anyone it will come back to them one day. Sometimes the wrong that they have done to others comes back double.

In the book of (Psalms 142) The Good News Bible and Today's Version

A Prayer for Help

I call to the Lord for help;
I plead with him.
I bring him all my complaints
I tell him all my troubles.
When I'm ready to give up,
He knows what I should do.
In the path where I walk,
My enemies have hidden a trap for me.
When I look beside me,
I see that there is no one to help me,

No one to protect me.
No one cares for me.
Lord I cry to you for help;
You, Lord are my protector,
You are all I want in this life.
Listen to my cry for help,
For I am sunk in despair,
Save me from my enemies;
They are too strong for me.
Set me free from my distress,"
Then in the assembly of your people
I will praise you
Because of your goodness to me.

David was a man after Gods own heart because He recognized God as Sovereign ruler of every aspect of creation, Perfect Judge, and Lawgiver. When David sinned, which we all do) he understood that he had sinned against God, and in this understanding, he was grieved in his own heart and he repented. He humbled himself under the mighty hand of God. God wants us all to be like David, to recognize our rebellious ways and to turn from them, back to Him by way of the cross; joining ourselves to the death and resurrection of Jesus Christ, Gods Son, by faith (believing and trusting). For the removing of sin and rebirth into the kingdom of God where His will, for perfect justice, peace and love abide forever and can never again be challenged by rebellion, which at the cross was done away with, as our wills were gladly conformed to God's in Christ.

David prayed many times for protection, help, healing, prosperity, enemies, restoration, favor, repentance, and deliverance. There are people that are in bondage who do wrong and they like it. They are many in prison because they don't want to change or be free. Sometimes fear comes in and we are afraid to make that change in our life. There is hope for you. You can be the individual that wants you to be. There are souls out there in the world that God wants you to help set free from the enemy. How can you help someone when you are not free to serve God? My question to you today is; Do you want to be free from sin? You need to ask God to come into your life in the name of Jesus and show you a better way to live. You cannot fight Satan, his demons, imps and legions by yourself. Jesus defeated Satan and he has the keys of Hell and Death. That's my Big brother and yours too, if you turn your life over to him.

John saw Jesus in the Spirit on the Lord's Day and the Lord Jesus ministered to him personally and told him not to be afraid. John spent time with Jesus and he knew him and his ways. There was no fault in Jesus. He had compassion on the sinners as well as the saints of God. John said Revelation 1 in verse 17 that Jesus laid his hands on him, saying to him, (Fear not; I am the first and the last.)

Revelation 1:9-17

1:9   I John, who also am your brother, and companion in tribulation, and in the kingdom and patience of Jesus Christ, was in the isle that is called Patmos, for the word of God, and for the testimony of Jesus Christ.

1:10   I was in the Spirit on the Lord's day, and heard behind me a great voice, as of a trumpet.

1:11   Saying, I am Alpha and Omega, the first and the last: and, What thou seest, write in a book, and send it unto the seven churches which are in Asia; unto Ephesus, and unto Smyrna, and unto Pergamos, and unto Thyatira, and unto Sardis, and unto Philadelphia, and unto Laodicea.

1:12   And I turned to see the voice that spake with me. And being turned, I saw seven golden candlesticks;

1:13   And in the midst of the seven candlesticks one like unto the Son of man, clothed with a garment down to the foot, and girt about the pap's with a golden girdle.

1:14   His head and his hairs were white like wool, as white as snow; and his eyes were as a flame of fire;

1:15   And his feet like unto fine brass, as if they burned in a furnace; and his voice as the sound of many waters.

1:16   And he had in his right hand seven stars: and out of his mouth went a sharp two edged sword: and his countenance was as the sun shineth in his strength.

1:17   And when I saw him, I fell at his feet as dead. And he laid his right hand upon me, saying unto me, Fear not; I am the first and the last:

In the book (**Matthew 16:19**) God spoke to Peter and told him that He would give him the keys of the kingdom of heaven, **and whatever he bound on earth would be bound, and whatever He loosed on earth would be loosed in heaven.**

Hell's gates, which have imprisoned people and put them into bondage, cannot stand God's Church moving against it in kingdom authority. Jesus gave his followers authority, or control to the Church to bind and loose on earth. Jesus has given us the keys to his kingdom power to stop evil and release God's power on different situations. It is the anointing power of Jesus Christ. We must use the authority of God's word to break the gates of hell and set people free in the name of Jesus.

bind- power to stop, forbid loose- release, or permit

We must read the Word of God which is the Bible to know what God says about a situation or circumstance. There are instructions on every box, bag or carton to tell you what you need to make it work. Read all the instructions or you will mess something up and will not be able to use what you brought or what someone else has given you. Satan doesn't want you to know the instructions about your trials, tribulations and test to make them work for your good. He doesn't want you to know the authority or power you have in Jesus Christ.

(Hosea 4:6) My people are destroyed for lack of knowledge; because thou have rejected knowledge, I will also reject thee, that thou shalt be no priest to me; seeing thou hast forgotten the law of thy God, I will also forget thy children. I don't know about you but, I want me, my seed, and my grandchildren to be delivered and blessed. I know they will have testimonies when God deliver them. When they call on him, I want him to answer them.

Pray this prayer knowing that you want to be free from doing what you used to do that was wrong. You can know that changing your life toward God is peace. You'll have peace knowing that you and others are in God's hands.

Prayer

Lord in the name of Jesus I want me to be free from bondage in the flesh, so that I can be a vessel of honor for you. Give me a desire to want to change and treat others right. Help me to pray for myself and others that are going through the same temptations that I'm going thru. I want my life to change for myself, my family, and that you may bring out the best in me. I know that someone will then look at my life and want to change their life around. I want to read your word to get wisdom, knowledge and understanding. I want to be better and not bitter. I don't want to be in bondage in any way. Lord I know that I don't have to be in jail or prison to be in bondage, I can be living at home and not be free. Please keep me so that I may be loosed from any way of thinking that is not in your will. I want to be free in Christ Jesus and have peace in my life. Thank you Lord! **In Jesus Name! Amen**

Chapter Five

THE SACRIFICES OF GOD
ARE A BROKEN SPIRIT

There are times in your life that you will feel as though you want to cry. Sometimes it seems that no one cares about you. We as a human race have not spent a lot of time reading God's Word, will feel despair or lowly at heart. We may think that there is no way out of our circumstances. Those of you who will cry and talk to God and be sincere about what you are saying to God will be victorious in our circumstances. There is an answer to all that you have been through, and all that you will have to go through to get to your destiny. God cares about you and he is concerned. I know that you are saying that if God can fix my situation, why doesn't he do it? I don't know the answer why he will not fix every situation or problem at this time, but there is a reason why, because he has the power to do it.

I know that Jesus was faced with some problems and he did not even help himself. There was a reason for him not using his power to free himself from the cross at Calvary. We're glad today that Jesus did not free himself from the cross so that we can have everlasting life.

We must continue to listen to other positive testimonies and encourage ourselves to wait on God. **(Psalms 51:17) says; the sacrifices of God are a broken spirit; a broken and a contrite heart, O God thou wilt not despise. God loves us to cry when we have problems in our life because it keeps us humble. When we stay humble our** prayers are pure and sincere. **God moves speedily for us because he knows that there is truth in our communication with him.**

David knew how to move God with repentance and brokenness. When you know that you have offended God and not walked according to His Word, you are out of fellowship with God. David knew that the fellowship that he had with God was precious and he cried out to God and wanted restored fellowship with him. David confessed his sins and repented all the time and God forgave him and purged his sins. David knew what it was like to have joy and restoration from God. The presence of God, which is the Holy Spirit, can work on his behalf in his life.

The best sacrifice that we can give God is being humble and broken before him. Crying out to him and letting him know that we are sorry for our mistakes and doing things the wrong way. **(John 11:35) Jesus wept.** Jesus cried before God because he was hurt that Lazarus was dead. In **(John 11:22)** Martha told Jesus, **"But I know, that even now, whatsoever thou wilt ask of God, God will give it thee.** Martha knew that Jesus had a personal relationship with God. She knew that Jesus was living a life that was pleasing to God. She had seen many miracles that Jesus had done through Father God. Verse 23 Jesus told Martha, **"Thy brother shall rise again."** Jesus knew that God would honor his request and raise up Lazarus. It's all right to shed tears. There are also tears of joy that can bless us. **Psalms 126:5, 6** This is a promise from God. **"Those that sow in tears shall reap in joy."** This means that people who are suffering, in pain, and crying because they may be going through something that they can do nothing about. Prayer, praise and worship will allow tears to be shed sometimes, so that we can receive healing from God. Prayer, praise and worship are powerful weapons against Spiritual Warfare. **God promise us that he will give us peace that surpasses all understanding.** In **Philippians 4:7** (The Word of God also says in **II Corinthians 10:4** says, **"For the weapons of our warfare are not carnal, but they are mighty through God to the pulling down of stronghold."** If you want your family to be delivered from Satan's strongholds, ask God to do it for you and thank him that it will be done for you or whoever you are praying for.

While animals do not cry in the way that humans do, they do produce tears. Since tear production, called lacrimation, is necessary for healthy eyes, most vertebrates are capable of producing tears. Elephants, which are sensitive and highly intelligent animals with an evolved social structure, have been observed "crying." Charles Darwin was told by the keepers of Indian elephants at the London zoo that the animals shed tears from sorrow.

God knows that we are thankful for what he has brought us through trials, and when we are just pretending to be broken before him. Sometimes I think about the things that God has done for me and my family, it brings tears to my eyes because I could have been anywhere and also dead a long time ago. I'm saved, sanctified and filled with his precious Holy Spirit. That's an awesome testimony because it brings tears of joy to my eyes. God chose me as one of his witnesses for him. Thank you Jesus, Hallelujah!!! Amen!

Prayer

Father God, in the name of Jesus I am asking you to forgive me from all my sins. I am asking you to keep me humble and broken before you because Psalms 51 chapter says **a humble and contrite spirit you will not despise.** I stay in repentance before you because I may think a wrong thought, or say something that is out of your will. You might have told me to do something and I did not do it your way. I may think I'm right when I say something and could be wrong. Thank you for hearing my prayers and answering them. In Jesus name I pray. Amen

Chapter Six

UNANSWERED PRAYERS

Sometimes God's greatest gift is unanswered prayers, because as a human race we ask for things that we don't need sometimes. I am reminded of a movie that came on television that the guy in the picture wanted his high school sweetheart back into his life and he always wanted to marry her. The high school sweetheart came back into his life after he was older and married. It was about twenty years later. He thought that God had answered his prayers and brought her back to him even though he had married and had a teenage son. He found out that the high school sweetheart had many relationships with other men. At the end of the picture his Wife and her met and they began to talk. His wife asked her did she still love her husband from a teenager until now. She replied; she loved all her men. This woman was not going to be a faithful wife to him if he had married her. The Lord did not answer his prayers. The wife he had was best for him. He was married when the high school sweetheart came back home to visit. In the end of the movie he realized that he had married a faithful women and he accepted that. He thanked God for unanswered prayers because he would have endured heartaches if he had married his high school sweetheart and probably divorced.

I am reminded of myself when I was working and I saw other children dressed nice for the Holidays but at the time I could not buy new clothing for my children every Holiday. I was a single working parent and I had to pay car note, house note, and insurances, buy food, or pay for medical insurance and other insurances. I found out later on in life that the person was getting money the wrong way, I asked God to forgive me for wanting what another person had. I thank God that he did not answer my prayers because I might have a prison record for doing things that was not legal or right. If God had given you everything that you asked for in life you may be in worse trouble, heartaches, pain, and have no peace or joy today.

We know that sometimes God gives us our desires, **(Psalms 37:4)** **(Philippians 4:19)** our needs, and our wants. **(Psalms23:1)** We still have to be careful what we ask God for. Our prayers should ask God whatever he knows that is best for us in every situation that we pray about. **(Matthew 6:9-13)** This is the model prayer that we all should pray. Not some of the time, but all the time.

⁹ After this manner therefore pray ye: Our Father which art in heaven, Hallowed be thy name.

¹⁰ Thy kingdom come, Thy will be done in earth, as it is in heaven.

¹¹ Give us this day our daily bread.

¹² And forgive us our debts, as we forgive our debtors.

¹³ And lead us not into temptation, but deliver us from evil: For thine is the kingdom, and the power, and the glory, forever. Amen.

Verse 8 says "Be not ye therefore like unto them: for your Father knoweth what things ye have need of, before you ask him.

We ask for things or someone in life that God knows is not our mate. You cannot force anyone to love you or accept you for who you are. You must be willing to change your life around for yourself and God. If you try to change for someone other than you it won't last too long. You don't want anger or bitterness to break up any friendship.

I could have allowed myself to get into trouble in order to give my children everything they wanted or I wanted them to have. My income at that time and my finances were limited with the job that I had. There are consequences to every wrong step we make in life. Today they could have been without a mother if I had made wrong choices in that situation. I thank God for me making the right choice.

In the book of **Judges 11:30-31** says;

And Jephthah vowed a vow unto the Lord, and said, if thou shalt without fail deliver the children of Ammon into mine hands.

Then it shall be, that whatsoever cometh forth of the doors of my house to meet me, when I return in peace from the children of Ammon, shall surely be the lord's and I will offer it up for a burnt offering.

I know that Jephthah wished that God wouldn't have answered his request ever.

Verse 34 says, "And Jephthah came to Mizpeh unto his house, and behold, his daughter came out to meet him with timbrels and with dances: and she was his only child: beside her he had neither son nor daughter.

35. And it came to pass, when he saw her, that he rent his clothes, and said, Alas, my daughter! Thou hast brought me very low, and thou art one of them that trouble me: for I have opened my mouth unto the Lord, and I cannot go back.

36 And she said unto him, My father, if thou hast opened thy mouth unto the Lord, do to me according to that which hath proceeded out of thy mouth; forasmuch as the Lord hath taken vengeance for thee of thine enemies, even of the children of Ammon.

37 And she said unto her father, Let this thing be done for me: let me alone two months, that I may go up and down upon the mountains, and bewail my virginity, I and my fellows.

38 And he said, Go. And he sent her away for two months: and she went with her companions, and bewailed her virginity upon the mountains.

39 And it came to pass at the end of two months, that she returned unto her father, who did with her according to his vow which he had vowed: and she knew no man. And it was a custom in Israel.

40 That the daughters of Israel went yearly to lament the daughter of Jephthah the Gileadite four days in a year.

God allowed Jephthah daughter more time to spend with herself and her father. God could have taken her the first day that she came out of her house in an instance.

In the book of **Matthew 26:39-42**

³⁹ And he went a little farther, and fell on his face, and prayed, saying, O my Father, if it be possible, let this cup pass from me: nevertheless not as I will, but as thou wilt.

⁴⁰ And he cometh unto the disciples, and findeth them asleep, and saith unto Peter, What, could ye not watch with me one hour?

⁴¹ Watch and pray, that ye enter not into temptation: the spirit indeed is willing, but the flesh is weak.

⁴² He went away again the second time, and prayed, saying, O my Father, if this cup may not pass away from me, except I drink it, thy will be done.

Jesus was beaten, whipped, and bled for our sins. He also was nailed to the cross and pierced in the side for us; that we might become the righteousness of God in Him. Jesus said nevertheless not as I will. (But as thou will). In verse **39** Jesus did not want to separate from the Lord. Jesus became sin for us. Verse **42** Jesus says; Lord if you won't take this cup from me except I go through whatever I have to go through, thy will be done. God could have kept Jesus from going to the cross for our sins and then we would not have a mediator today. Jesus stood in the gap for our sins. We should thank God for some prayers being unanswered because only he knows what is best for us.

I thank God, Jesus did not come off the cross and he did not ask the host of heaven to help him. Also I thank God for allowing him to drink the bitter cup for the whole world so that we can be saved and filled with the Holy Spirit. Jesus see us as totally righteous people before God. God forgives us of our sins, failures, and shortcomings, because of the shed blood of our Lord and Savior Jesus Christ. Satan did not want Jesus blood to be shed for our remission of sins. We can go to God and not feeling guilty, unworthy, or condemned. We can repent and be reconciled to God. Can you think of some of the prayers that you thank God for not answering? Can you think of some of the things that you thank God for not giving you? Get a piece of paper and a pencil and write them down and meditate on them for approximately five minutes. Praise God for unanswered prayers according to his will. **(1 Corinthians 1:27) But God had chosen the foolish things of the world to confound the wise; and God hath chosen the weak things of the world to confound the things which are mighty.**

Prayer

Father in the name of Jesus I come before you asking that you please forgive me of all my sins. I pray that your will be done in my life and I know that Romans 8:26-27 say that the Holy Spirit who is a person will make intercession for me according to the will of God. I don't know every prayer or everything that I should ask or pray for. Thank you Lord, for not answering all of my prayers that I have prayed. I thank you for not coming off the cross. I thank you for suffering on Calvary for our sins. I thank you for being Lord and Savior in our lives today. In Jesus' name, Amen!

Chapter Seven

TRUST IN THE LORD

We may think that every prayer that we pray should be answered by God. It seems foolish to pray and not get your prayers answered. God says he takes the foolish things to confound the wise. No matter what our plans, desires, needs, and wants are, God has to bless them.

In the book of (Proverbs 16:9) **a man's heart deviseth his way: but the Lord directed his steps**. We can make plans or decisions for ourselves, but if the Lord doesn't direct our steps it will not work. Anything that we do or chose in this life should be directed by God. There is victory and blessings when God is in any situation or circumstance. There is an old saying "little is much when God is in it."

There comes a time in life when our backs are up against the wall. We think that there are problems that just can't be solved. What I'm saying is that we have to trust in the Lord. Sometimes in life there seem like it is no way out of a trial, test or hard times.

There is a way out if you talk to the Lord and allow him to minister to you. You must get quiet before him and listen. There are three things that you must do for victory in any situation.

- You must confess your sins to the Lord.
- Ask the Lord for forgiveness.
- Thank him for what he's going to do.

I found out in my Christian experience with salvation in the Lord Jesus Christ that I had a powerful weapon to fight Satan with. The devil can't stand praise and worship toward God because he was a worshipper and praiser God and became jealous of God.

(Isaiah14:12) How art thou fallen from heaven, O Lucifer, son of the morning! how art thou cut down to the ground, which didst weaken the nations! (Isaiah 14:13-14) For thou hast said in thine heart, I will ascend into Heaven, I will exalt my throne above the stars of God: I will sit also upon the mount of the congregation, in the sides of the north: (Verse 14) I will ascend above the heights of the clouds; I will be like the most High.

Lucifer who is Satan does not want you to have victory in any situation. If you can praise God for what he's doing in your situation, then and only then you will have a testimony.

I don't know the answer to many questions why God allow some things to happen, but I know that he is still God.

(Psalms 24:1-6)

1. The earth is the Lord's, and the fullness thereof; the world, and they that dwell therein. 2. For he hath founded it upon the seas, and established it upon the floods. 3. Who shall ascend into the hill of the Lord? Or who shall stand in his holy place? 4. He that hath clean hands, and a pure heart; who hath not lifted up his soul unto vanity, nor sworn deceitfully. 5. He shall receive the blessing from the Lord, and righteousness from God of his salvation. 6. This the generation of them that seek him, that seek thy face. O Jacob. Selah. God found and established the earth and Satan does not like that. As long as we are willing vessels we will be used by God. God created us in his likeness also.

If you will be obedient in reading God's word and go to church service eventually you will learn to trust God in situations and circumstances. There will be powerful testimonies told at times to strengthen you and your family. There are people that have endured more hardships than you and are still worshipping God. Those of you, who are incarcerated and can go to the service inside the unit, please do so. You will understand why God allowed you to come there. Many of you God protected you in your mess and he would not allow Satan to take your life. Every one that is living knows at least one person that is saved and trusting God for their families and loved ones to be delivered from some type of bondage. Most of all you must develop a love for God to trust him. He wants you to come out of bondage from the enemy and separate yourselves and be blessed. The Holy Spirit wants to give you total deliverance and blessing from God.

There is nothing that can take the place of God or Christ in your life. God loves us and he wants you to allow him to give you a Holy Ghost takeover.

Philippians 4:7 says; "And the peace of God, Which passeth all understanding, shall keep your hearts and minds through Christ Jesus."

The bible is true and everything you need to know is in the Word of God about being a Christian. You have to be willing to fight the adversary with prayer, fasting and reading the word. When we worship and praise God and tell him how awesome He is. You can worship God in tithes and offering also if you have it. It's time for women and men to walk right with God, talk right, and live right. If you haven't gotten their yet, ask God to help you. You must trust God for yourself.

The Bible tells me in the book of **Jeremiah 7:8** Behold, ye trust in lying words that cannot profit.

Jeremiah 9:4 Take ye heed every one of his neighbor and trust ye not in any brother: for every brother will utterly supplant, and every neighbor will walk with slanders.

Micah 7:5 Trust ye not in a friend, put ye not confidence in a guide: keep the doors of thy mouth from her that lieth in thy bosom.

Mark 10:24 And the disciples were astonished at his words. But Jesus answereth again, and saith unto them, Children, how hard is it for them that trust in richest to enter into the kingdom of God.

2 Corinthians1:9-10 (9) But we had the sentence of death in ourselves that we should not trust in ourselves, but in God which raiseth the dead:

(10) Who delivered us from so great a death, and doth deliver: in whom we <u>trust</u> that he will yet deliver us;

I Timothy 4:8-10 (8) For bodily exercise profiteth little: but godliness is profitable unto all things, having promise of the life that now is, and of that which is to come. (9) This is a faithful saying and worthy of all acceptation. (10) For therefore we both labour and suffer reproach, because we <u>trust</u> in the living God, who is the Saviour of all men, especially of those that believe.

Psalms 112:7 He shall not be afraid of evil tidings: his heart is fixed, <u>trusting in the Lord.</u>

Your heart has to be fixed in order for you to trust in the Lord.

Galatians 6:1-18

Men and women need to do the right thing to make things successful for them and their families. You may need help sometimes, but you will still need to pray and trust God..

Brethren, if a man be overtaken in a fault, ye which are spiritual, restore such a one in the spirit of meekness; considering thyself, lest thou also be tempted. ² Bear ye one another's burdens, and so fulfil the law of Christ. ³ For if a man think himself to be something, when he is nothing, he deceiveth himself. ⁴<u>But let every man prove his own work, and then shall he have rejoicing in himself alone, and not in another.</u> ⁵ For every man shall bear his own burden. ⁶ Let him that is taught in the word communicate unto him that teacheth in all good things.⁷<u>Be not deceived; God is not mocked: for whatsoever a man soweth, that shall he also reap.</u> ⁸ For he that soweth to his flesh shall of the flesh reap corruption; but he that soweth to the Spirit shall of the Spirit reap life everlasting. ⁹ And let us not be weary in well doing: for in due season we shall reap, if we faint not. ¹⁰ As we have therefore opportunity, let us do good unto all men, especially unto them who are of the household of faith.¹¹ Ye see how large a letter I have written unto you with mine own hand. ¹² As many as desire to make a fair shew in the flesh, they constrain

**you to be circumcised; only lest they should suffer persecution
for the cross of Christ. ¹³ For neither they themselves who are
circumcised keep the law; but desire to have you circumcised, that
they may glory in your flesh.¹⁴ But God forbid that I should glory,
save in the cross of our Lord Jesus Christ, by whom the world is
crucified unto me, and I unto the world.
¹⁵ For in Christ Jesus neither circumcision availeth anything,
nor uncircumcision, but a new creature. ¹⁶ And as many as walk
according to this rule, peace be on them, and mercy, and upon the
Israel of God. ¹⁷ From henceforth let no man trouble me: for I bear
in my body the marks of the Lord Jesus. ¹⁸ Brethren, the grace of
our Lord Jesus Christ be with your spirit. Amen.**

Look at verse **2** and **5** "It's alright to help someone else in verse **2**,
but in verse 5 says they must help themselves also. There are people who
can get a job, training skills to work, or to open a business. There is
always something a person can do to help themselves financially make
money legally. The scripture is talking about those that help themselves.

One of my favorite scriptures is **Proverbs 3:5 Trust in the Lord
with all thine heart; and lean not unto thine own understanding.
(6) In all thy ways acknowledge him, and he shall direct thy paths.**
I needed a loan and I had already been to the Credit Union once and
they told me to come back in six months. I stood on **Mark 11:22-23**
and it says;

And Jesus answering saith unto them, Have faith in God. Verse 23
says; **For verily I say unto you, That whosoever shall say unto this
mountain, Be thou removed and be thou cast into the sea; and shall
not doubt in his heart, but shall believe that those things which he
saith shall come to pass; he shall have whatsoever he saith.**

First of all I repented for all my sins and I was sincere about what
I said. I commanded poverty to be cast in the sea and it was that
mountain in my life, because I needed some money for me and my three
children. So I went back to the Credit Union in a week and they told
me that I needed to come back in six months and they told me we have
already talked to you about this before. They said that we explained it
to you, and then the Manager of the Credit Union walked in and heard

the conversation. He told the loan officer to give me what I wanted and he would sign the loan. **Thank you Jesus!**

If I didn't trust God and go back to the Credit Union and stand on the Word of God I would not have gotten the loan. I had the authority to command everything that was stopping me from getting the loan. I spoke the word and stood on the word. Bad credit had to be cast in the sea also. You must trust the Lord and also his word. There are many scriptures in the Bible about trusting in God. He also is saying that you can't be proud and put your trust in him at the same time. None of us have it all together: the rich, middle class or the poor.

This is a testimony; I was buying a Dodge custom van fully loaded. My finances got out of order and I had to return the van back to the dealership. I call the Dodge dealership to come and get the van. They eventually came and repossessed it. I asked God for forgiveness for not having my finances in order. The book of Proverbs 3:6 In all thy ways acknowledge him, and he shall direct thy paths. I had not sought God in spending after I started buying a van truck. I went to the Credit Union after I repented and they looked on my Credit report and seen that I had purchased a van.

They said that it was paid in full. I assumed that someone else brought it from the dealer. Anyway the Credit union loaned me fifteen thousand to purchase another vehicle and that was in 1995. One year later the check that I paid down on the car for the title and taxes came back to me because the dealership closed.

We all need to trust the lord with every breath that we breathe and everything that we have; even our children are just given to us for an appointed time. Our loved ones and friends also, that's why we should cherish our moments together. Every minute, every second and every hour of the day we must love people and life and thank God for it. **Amen and Amen!!**

One of the **Psalms is Chapter 56** that says; **Be merciful unto me, O God: for man would swallow me up; he fighting daily oppresseth me.**[2] **Mine enemies would daily swallow me up: for they be many that fight against me, O thou most High.**[3] **What time I am afraid, I will trust in thee.**[4] **In God I will praise his word, in God I have put my trust; I will not fear what flesh the can do unto me.**[5] **Every day they wrest my words: all their thoughts are against me for evil.**[6] **They gather themselves together, they hide themselves, they**

mark my steps, when they wait for my soul.[7] Shall they escape by iniquity? in thine anger cast down the people, O God.[8] Thou tellest my wanderings: put thou my tears into thy bottle: are they not in thy book?[9] When I cry unto thee, then shall mine enemies turn back: this I know; for God is for me.[10] In God will I praise his word: in the LORD will I praise his word.[11] In God have I put my trust: I will not be afraid what man can do unto me.[12] Thy vows are upon me, O God: I will render praises unto thee.[13] For thou hast delivered my soul from death: wilt not thou deliver my feet from falling, that I may walk before God in the light of the living?

Faith becomes strong and it grows through trusting in the Lord. The starting point is the Word of God. (The Bible) there are a lot of Bibles in the world today, so be sure it is the true Word of God, nothing taking from it. The meaning should be the same. Many people want to trust in a God that they can see. I f He was here he would not last because all of us would want a piece of him or to touch him at the same time.

Because you can't see him, but you can feel his presence when you develop a relationship with Jesus. He can be everywhere at the same time. Choose to act on God's Word. If you read the Bible you may not understand everything at once. Little by little he will give you golden nuggets of His Word and as you read it write down what you feel He's ministering to you. The Holy Spirit will touch your heart on what to write down.

You may know someone who was convicted of a crime that they did not commit. Every one incarcerated is not guilty, but only God and you know the truth. Try not to be angry about it, because you can trust God and talk to him for his will to be done in that person's life. Let God be the avenger, because **Romans 12:19** says; Dearly beloved, avenge not yourselves, but rather give place unto wrath: for it is written, **Vengeance is mine; I will repay saith the Lord.**

Psalms 55:22 says; Cast thy burden upon the Lord, and he shall sustain thee: He shall never suffer the righteous to be moved. Praise God for the victory and never ever give up on God.

Psalms 40:1-4

1 I waited patiently for the LORD; and he inclined unto me, and heard my cry. **2** He brought me up also out of an horrible pit, of the miry clay, and set my feet upon a rock, and established my goings. **3** And he hath put a new song in my mouth, even praise unto our God: many shall see it, and fear, and shall trust in the LORD. **4** Blessed is that man that maketh the LORD his trust, and respecteth not the proud, nor such as turn aside to lies.

Prayer

Father in the name of Jesus, I come before you asking you to forgive me. Help me to trust you for everything that I need. Forgive me for not trusting you in every situation and not calling upon you to help me. I need to stay up under your umbrella of protection. Help me to do and say the right things in this life. I will trust you at all times and your praise shall continually be in my mouth. I will trust you in the salvation of my family and myself. Thank you for hearing my prayers in Jesus name. Amen!

Chapter Eight

PROTECTING YOUR ANOINTING

When you read God's word with sincerity, there should be a seed that should be planted in your heart that makes you want to be better and do good. Most of all it should make you want to get closer to God because you will find out that the word of God is true.

12 This is my commandment, That ye love one another, as I have loved you.

13 Greater love hath no man than this that a man lay down his life for his friends.

14 Ye are my friends, if ye do whatsoever I command you.

15 Henceforth I call you not servants; for the servant knoweth not what his lord doeth: but I have called you friends; for all things that I have heard of my Father I have made known unto you.

16 Ye have not chosen me, but I have chosen you, and ordained you, that ye should go and bring forth fruit, and that your fruit should remain: that whatsoever ye shall ask of the Father in my name, he may give it you.

17 These things I command you, that ye love one another.

18 If the world hate you, ye know that it hated me before it hated you.

19 If ye were of the world, the world would love his own: but because ye are not of the world, but I have chosen you out of the world, therefore the world hateth you.

20 Remember the word that I said unto you, The servant is not greater than his lord. If they have persecuted me, they will also persecute you; if they have kept my saying, they will keep yours also.

21 But all these things will they do unto you for my name's sake, because they know not him that sent me.

22 If I had not come and spoken unto them, they had not had sin: but now they have no cloak for their sin.

23 He that hateth me hateth my Father also.

24 If I had not done among them the works which none other man did, they had not had sin: but now have they both seen and hated both me and my Father.

25 But this cometh to pass, that the word might be fulfilled that is written in their law, They hated me without a cause.

26 But when the Comforter is come, whom I will send unto you from the Father, even the Spirit of truth, which proceedeth from the Father, he shall testify of me:

27 And ye also shall bear witness, because ye have been with me from the beginning.

When I was seeking the Lord and reading His Word, a couple of verses I kept hearing in my mind. One of them was **John 15:16**

I thought that I had chosen to come to God, but he had already chosen me to do his will. There are promises if you do God's will. John

14:14 and John 15:7 You will have an anointing on you when you stay close to Jesus. He will give you favor with him when you ask for something that you need. **That whatsoever ye shall ask of the Father in my name, that he may give it you.**

You must go and bring forth fruit, (telling others about Jesus Christ and him being crucified for our sins).

When you start doing God's will, everyone will not like you because flesh loves to do wrong. Continue to crucify the flesh by staying in

God's presence by talking to him and doing his will. Loving one another and helping others that need help. In the book of **John15:26** say that

<u>**The Comforter**</u> will come, who will be sent from the Father to help you. To do the things that will bless you and keep you in the will of God.

Even when you mess up the Holy Spirit will let you know that you need to repent and ask him to help you. The Holy Spirit is the anointing that you need to have God's favor on your life. There are many things and people in our lives that hinders and vexes us. Then we step out of line with what God wants to do for us and with us. <u>We don't protect the anointing that God has placed in our lives</u> and on us. Why? Because we decide to be people and self pleasers than God pleasers and we get right back into trouble and then we need God to help us get out of situations.

In the book of **Galatians 5:16-26**

16 This I say then, Walk in the Spirit, and ye shall not fulfil the lust of the flesh.

17 For the flesh lusteth against the Spirit, and the Spirit against the flesh: and these are contrary the one to the other: so that ye cannot do the things that ye would. The Spirit and the flesh are enemies one to another, because the flesh wants to do its own thing whether it is right or wrong and the Spirit is controlled by God and it is perfect.

18 But if ye be led of the Spirit, ye are not under the law.

19 Now the works of the flesh are manifest, which are these; Adultery, fornication, uncleanness, lasciviousness,

20 Idolatry, witchcraft, hatred, variance, emulations, wrath, strife, seditions, heresies,

21 Envyings, murders, drunkenness, revellings, and such like: of the which I tell you before, as I have also told you in time past, that they which do such things shall not inherit the kingdom of God.

22 But the fruit of the Spirit is love, joy, peace, longsuffering, gentleness, goodness, faith,

23 Meekness, temperance: against such there is no law.

24 And they that are Christ's have crucified the flesh with the affections and lusts.

25 If we live in the Spirit, let us also walk in the Spirit.

26 Let us not be desirous of vain glory, provoking one another, envying one another.

You have to be anointed and a new creature in Christ Jesus. God's presence will be with you and it energizes the person that it's upon. You have boldness like never before to confront a situation with the

Word of God that is in the Bible.

We must speak and believe the promises that God spoke to you, your children, and your children's children.

I asked God to allow me to feel his presence. I may be at home or driving the car. The anointing of God is awesome. I have felt the presence and power of God in my life. It is the anointing that comes when you are obedient to the will of God.

Ephesians 2:3-5

3 Among whom also we all had our conversation in times past in the lusts of our flesh, fulfilling the desires of the flesh and of the mind; and were by nature the children of wrath, even as others.

4 But God, who is rich in mercy, for his great love wherewith he loved us,
5 Even when we were dead in sins, hath quickened us together with Christ, (by grace ye are saved.

We all have had conversations that were not of God. We were fulfilling the desires and lust of the flesh. We were also allowing our sins to lead us astray from the will of God.

Verse 4 says that God is rich in mercy and he loves us with his great love. There are many scriptures in the Bible about God's mercy.

So therefore there is no excuse to not be anointed to do the will of God and to protect your anointing by repenting and doing better.

Isaiah 10:27 And it shall come to pass in that day, that his burden shall be taken away from off thy shoulder, and his yoke from off thy neck, and the yoke shall be destroyed because of the anointing. Isaiah was speaking of the Assyrian that had God's people in bondage and burden or upset. The Holy Spirit in our lives will release an anointing on us that will destroy satanic forces that comes against believers in the body of Christ. In **Psalms** that is one of the repentant scriptures that says; **Psalms 51:10 Create in me a clean heart, O God; and renew a right spirit within me.**

We need to ask God to continually give us a clean heart so that his anointing will stay with us. It destroys yokes and bondages that the devil wants to keep us from moving forward in our finances, wisdom, knowledge, and prosperity.

Satan does not want you to persevere in being blessed. When you need, want or desire something from God that's according to his will he hears us. The answer to the asking is yes and the Banks may say no. I would go back to the bank and stand on the Word of God. You know if you have sown seed in the kingdom of God mixed with faith it will grow.

Luke 6:38 Give and it shall be given unto you; good measure, pressed down, and shaken together and running over, shall men give unto your bosom. For with the measure ye mete it shall be measured to you again. I will be obedient and honor God's command to give because I have reaped harvests and will continue to be blessed financially.

1. **I will be a good steward of all he has and be blessed me with**
2. **I give cheerfully**
3. **I plant seed in good ground.**
4. **I will always try to remember to stay humble**

When God pays you back it may be thirty, sixty or hundred fold interest. I found out that you can't beat giving, no matter how you try. **Matthew 13:8 says; But other fell into good ground, and brought forth fruit, some a hundredfold, some sixtyfold, some thirtyfold.** I don't know about you but I thank and praise God and ask him for the hundredfold return to be a blessing for myself and someone else.

You must pray, read the Word and God will give you songs to sing that will help you to protect your anointing also. **Psalms 32:7 says; thou art my hiding place; thou shalt preserve me from trouble; thou shalt compass me about with songs of deliverance.(Selah) Psalms 32:8 says; I will instruct thee and teach thee in the way which thou shalt go: I will guide thee with mine eye.** The Song of Songs God give you to sing, Satan will move out of your way because he doesn't like it when you sing to God, That used to be his job or blessing.

If you protect your anointing by repenting and being godly sorrowful for doing wrong when the Holy Spirit convicts you.

When you feel that you have done something contrary to the will of God; repent. Your relationship with God will be assured, because we must never have the spirit of pride that we can't ask God for forgiveness.

John 10:10 says; The thief cometh not, but for to steal, and to kill, and to destroy; I am come that they might have life and that they might have it more abundantly.

Satan wants to destroy the anointing that is in your life and on your life. You cannot afford to let him do it. There are loved ones in your life that need yokes and bondages to be destroyed off their lives. When people know that you are anointed they will ask you to pray for them or someone. They need someone to stand in the gap for them. Jesus is standing in the gap for us also. He will not ask you to do something that he would not do.

Psalms 70

1. Make haste, O God, to deliver me; make haste to help me, O Lord. I want God to answer me speedily and quickly when I call upon him. Whoever I'm standing in the gap for or seeking the Lord for. I want to hear some powerful testimonies afterwards. Therefore I have to protect my anointing that God has placed on my life. I didn't understand how precious the anointing was at one time. When I repent when I pray God answers me. **Thank you Lord Jesus**

David in **Psalms 92:10** knew what it meant to be anointed **with** fresh oil. The anointing will protect you from your enemies.

In the book of **Judges 4**: Deborah a leader, judge, wife, prophetess, and military advisor had an anointing on her, She allowed the Spirit of God to shape her life. Barak did not want to go and fight Sisera without Deborah even though God told him to take ten thousand men. Barak wanted Deborah to go with him because she had an anointing on her of obedience and He knew the decisions that she made for people, God had to be with her. She had God's favor on her life. When you protect your anointing and keep it, you will see God's glory, honor, or highest respect given to you.

Judges 4:9 Deborah said, I will surely go with thee: notwithstanding the journey that thou takest shall not be for thine honour; for the Lord shall sell Sisera into the hand of a woman. And Deborah arose, and went with Barak to Kedesh.

If you want to receive the anointing of God and keep it, you can't compromise with wrong doing and sin. There must be a sincere love for God, Jesus and the Holy Spirit. Pray for the world and they that dwell there in.

Prayer

Father God, in the name of Jesus I come to you to ask for forgiveness for all my sin of omission, co-mission and I thank you for forgiving me. I come to you to ask you to keep me in your presence, and help me to be obedient to your will that the anointing that's on my life will help me and someone else to be strong in the Lord and in the power of your might. I thank you for your Word, prayer, fasting and giving me songs to sing when I'm going through some trial, tribulation or test. I know that you will direct my path. **In Jesus name, AMEN!**

Chapter Nine

HOLY GHOST ARREST

There are men, women, boys and girls who are under Holy Ghost arrest for something you done or for something you didn't do. Many of you were associated with the wrong person or persons. When God wants to get your attention to change your way of life or to seek him he will allow you to be where there is no distractions so that he can minister to you and you should trust him although you may be incarcerated.

Therefore, I call this Holy Ghost arrest because God wants your attention.

1 Corinthians 15:33) says "Be not deceived: <u>evil communications corrupt good manners</u>. If you are not strong enough to say no to doing anything that can harm you or someone else; you need to separate yourself from these people. When you get strong enough to say no to anything that will harm you or that is wrong, pray before you communicate with people that want to live in darkness.

Some of you are incarcerated, just gotten out of jail or may be on your way back to jail prison. You may be under Holy Ghost arrest because God wants to get your attention to turn from your way of living to his way, if you are living wrong.

Sometimes the Lord has to get you to himself where there will be no distractions or interference. We can repent and come clean before God and be true to what we are saying to God. Remember he already knows what you are going to say before you open your mouth. Many times I've told God if you help me get out of a situation, I will go to church. I would go for a while and then stop. It's easy to make vows to God. Do you know anyone that told God if you would do this for me, I will go to church and serve you? Sometimes people have good intentions but they are not ready to give their life to Christ. They know that they are only lying to God and themselves. One day that lie might turn into the truth. You will say what you mean and mean what you say.

As you began to study God's Word and meditate upon it, the golden treasures or nuggets that stay on your mind will be a blessing to you once again. It seems like I can't say that enough. Make sure that you have a pen and piece of paper because when a scripture stays with you and it touches your heart, you will certainly need to use it soon. Maybe the word is for a loved one, a friend, or enemy to encourage, rebuke or help them in some situation.

God is tired of the prison system being an **Adult Daycare Center**. Men and women who choose the wrong over the right or they don't care about the wrong that they are or were doing. The word of God says that sin is pleasure for a season..

Drinking and smoking constantly will cause you sometimes to crave for alcohol and cigarettes. When you are in distress or worrying it will cause you to want to smoke, drink or create bad habits. Stress will cause you to crave for things that will keep you from seeking God. Why? Because stress it is not from God. You must be aware of what's going on in your mind at all times.

In the book of **2 Corinthians 13:1**

This is the third time I am coming to you. In the mouth of two or three witnesses shall every word be established. The Lord will allow two or three people to tell you the same thing. Then you know that God is trying to tell you something. There were times when I was watching the gospel station on television and about three times they would say; "there's a book in you." I knew that it was conformation from God. I was reading about Malcolm X when he was an inmate in prison. He began to take the dictionary every day and learn words and their meaning. He made good out of the bad situation that he was in.

Nehemiah 13:2 says; because they met not the children of Israel with bread and water, but hired Balaam against them, that he should curse them: howbeit our God turned a curse into a blessing. It does not matter why you are in prison or jail. Repent to God and be true to yourself, because God knows everything. You cannot hide anything from God. He never sleeps and he is watching you and waiting on you to give him your best. When you are under Holy Ghost Arrest you know what you promised God that you would do. You made a vow to God to go to church and stay out of trouble. Temptation isn't hard to resist when you are not rooted and grounded in God's word. Christians and non-Christians are tempted and we all have to draw nigh to God.

James 4:7-8 says; Draw near to God and he will draw near to you.

Cleanse your hands, you sinners, and purify your hearts, you double-minded.

You know how much you want and need in your life. Some people do not want God to change their lives. The Holy Spirit will make some changes for the better. You will say to yourself "I wish I had given my life to Christ a long time ago.

Jail House Salvation

There are times when a person that is locked up behind bars, have been or is incarcerated feels that the only way they can get help from another Christian is being or acting Christ like. Therefore they say that they are reading the Word of GOD every day. Praying and seeking God's help for their lives. If they are in a bad situation at the time and they need things around them to be better or maybe a case dropped they need God. Sometimes they confess that they have found Christ and they are saved. They will quote some of the scriptures enough to fool someone to believe that they have changed and turned from their evil or wrong doing ways. When they get out of prison whether it be on parole or not, they forget about the Bible. They go to church for a while and then they stop completely. When they get into trouble sometimes they will start back going to church for a while. They stop reading the bible completely. This is called jail house salvation. They were saved when they were in prison, jail or out on bond. They do not want or need God because they are out of the bad situation they were in or God has given them a miracle. God sees everything and he knows all things.

Prayer

Lord I come to you for forgiveness of my sin. I thank you that I am under Holy Ghost Arrest to read your word, repent and meditate with no distractions from my friends and family. You can speak to me and I will hear you. Anoint my ears to hear what you are saying to me.

Ephesians 6:10-10 tells me that I am in spiritual warfare daily and I need salvation, faith, peace, truth, and the word of God to win this war in this place and be set free spiritually and mentally and physically. Thank you Lord for delivering me from the hand of all my enemies. Help me to pass all tests. I want my love for you to be real.

Chapter Ten

OBEDIENCE

In this chapter I wanted scriptures only so that group discussions could be done together and speak on the sixty-six verses that I found in obeying or obedience. So I was willing to let it be omitted out of this book. I was going to do it in my next book if God would put it back on my heart. Over the weekend it bothered me to leave it out. Obeying is a word that we all wish we did not have to do all the time. Sometimes is okay, but not all the time.

Ephesians 6:1 Children, <u>obey</u> your parents <u>in the Lord</u>: for this is right. God wants us to obey our parents if they are telling us to do things that are right. We know that all of the parents in the world are not saved or want to do everything right. I have not be saved and delivered all my life. It's hard because many of us as children want to please our parents. You must pray for them when you come in the knowledge of the truth. I am talking about right or wrong things in life to do or not to do. Pray before you speak to a parent about what's going on in your life. Ask God to come in the conversation and intervene and be a mediator for all of you. Allow God to surround the conversations with the spirit of love.

Job 36:12 But if they <u>obey</u> not, they shall perish by the sword, and they shall die without <u>knowledge</u>. Knowing right from wrong and doing it is knowledge. Everyone needs knowledge every minute, every second, and every hour of the day. In the book of **Hosea 4:6 My people are destroyed for lack of knowledge. Because you have rejected**

knowledge, I will reject you from being priest for Me. Because you have forgotten the law of your God, I also will forget your children. The word of God is saying that if we don't want to obey the word of God we will be a disaster and evil done in our lives and our family. In God's obedience there will be mercy and truth. We need to know how to be blessed and happy in this life. The world is full of chaos because there is lack of God's principles. We have to seek God's guidance and wisdom today for ourselves and our family.

Romans 6:16 Know ye not, that to whom ye yield yourselves servants to <u>obey</u>**, his servants ye are to whom ye** <u>obey</u>**; whether of sin unto death, or of obedience unto righteousness.** If you want to be a servant of God, you must yield to God's will and read his word and obey him. Keep company or hang around people that desire to do well. **1 Corinthians 15:33 Do not be deceived: Evil company corrupts good habits.** I know this scripture is very true. You can't be around a person that is not delivered or saved and not do something wrong. You can stay around a curser all the time and eventually foul language will come out of your mouth. I don't understand it but, it has happened to me.

Romans Chapter 2 God is the righteous Judge and we must keep a forgiving heart toward each other and God. He offers eternal life to those who continually does well and obeys his word. He also promises glory, honor and peace. People will trust you and honor you, they see the love for God all over your character. The way you talk and your radiant smile. The joy of the Lord will be all over your appearance also.

In order for us to function the way God created for us to be and do, we must obey the word of God. It helps us financially, socially, and politically if we would ever run for office in the media. I know that sometimes it seems as though that others wants control over our lives. We are being picked on like penguins. It may not be true but it seems like that. What are you supposed to do when situations in your life like this happens? I would pray to God and ask him if I am the problem, show me how to get right. If my problem is the man or woman that I feel that has or is misusing me, help them to realize that they are wrong. Wait until God reveals it to you and them.

I Samuel 15:23 So Samuel said: Has the lord has great delight in burnt offerings and sacrifices. As obeying the voice of the Lord? Behold, to obey is better than sacrifice, And to heed than the fat

of rams. When God says that obeying his word, and his voice is better than any sacrifice that you can give him, which is love. What if your sacrifice is money and you want God to have some of it but, I'm going to continue doing what I want to do. God is saying keep your money because, I want you to be blessed first in obedience, then bring the sacrifice. I want to use you and anoint you to help someone else because you are obeying my word and taking heed to the wrong that I want to change in your life. God wants you to smile instead of looking mean and hateful. What will it cost you to smile?

I don't think it will cost us anything to smile sometimes. **Proverbs 15:13-14 says that; A merry heart makes a cheerful countenance. But the sorrow of the heart the spirit is broken. Verse 14 says; The heart of him who has understanding seeks knowledge, But he who is of a merry heart has continual feast.** The word of God says that you can acquire knowledge through obedience. Another way is that you can ask God for it.

There are two voices that we can obey. God gives you a free will to make a choice. Satan will eventually destroy you and allow you to think that you are getting away with the wrong that you are doing. God will bless you and forgive you, then you will become a peculiar treasure for him. **Exodus 19:5 says Now therefore, if ye ill <u>obey</u> my voice indeed, and keep my covenant, then shall you be a <u>peculiar</u> treasure unto me above all people: for all the earth is mine.**

You will not know God's voice unless you communicate with him or read his word. He speaks through leaders and others. The Holy Spirit is powerful and anointed. It is also sharp and it will dissect and cut you spiritually. Sometimes I have to say ouch because something that was said was for me to get correction. We only want to hear what makes us feel good at all times. We all make mistakes in life. Let the word clean, change our lives, and most of all lead us to repentance. **Hebrew 4:12 says; For the word of God is living and powerful, and sharper than any two-edged sword, piercing even to the division of soul and spirit, and of joints and, and is a discerner of the thoughts and intents of the heart. 2 Timothy 3:16 says that; All Scripture is given by inspiration of God, and is profitable for doctrines, for reproof, for correction, for instruction in righteousness.**

God is asking for obedience today like never before. We are going to have to come together and pray and seek his face. We need to know what

God wants us to do. The time is at hand and we cannot procrastinate with time or our lives. We must be very serious about everything that concerns us. Most of all we have to ask God to give us the Agape love to help one another.

There are many scriptures in obedience in the Bible, so therefore you need to pray and ask God for wisdom, knowledge and understanding. It is good to read the whole chapter and see what the scripture is talking about.

Colossians 3:20 says children; obey your parents in all things. In verse ten it says to put on the new man that is renewed in knowledge after the image of him that created him. You will have to know that God wants love and peace in your life today. You must know right from wrong.

If a parent teaches their child to do wrong God will hold them accountable for that. That same wicked deed or deeds that you use to hurt others will come back and hurt you or trouble you.

Use these scriptures for bible study and have an open discussion if you can. Let the golden nuggets and the treasure come out of the **Bible** or the **Word** of God and the Holy Spirit will bless you like never before. Receive the knowledge, wisdom and understanding that you need in everyday life.

As you read the scriptures, also read the chapters to get a better understanding of the **Word** of God. You also can have seminars, bible study and group discussions for empowerment.

I pray that God will open your understanding that you might understand the scriptures. (**Luke 24:45**)

Have group discussions on the obedience scriptures and give some to someone for bible study or at home and take notes as the Holy Spirit will bring revelation to you and the group or persons.

Ezekiel 3:3 Let the words of obey as we are focusing on this chapter be as honey in sweetness in your mouth. Read it until you can memorize some of the scriptures.

Enjoy!!!!

Prayer

Father I thank you that there are blessings, deliverance, healing, promises, power, love and miracles in obeying the word of GOD. I pray that through obedience of your word that many miracles will happen in my family, home and business. Help me to obey your voice and know the truth about how gracious you are. I thank you through obedience that you will give me dreams and visions of your will for my life. I also thank you for allowing your Holy Spirit to abide in me and be that comforter that I need. You promised me that I would be willing and obedient I shall eat the good of the land. I am ready to do what is right and prosper in a mighty way. My mind is made up; and I will not turn aside and do what is wrong. I know that there are others watching me to see if I am real in my walk and talk. Help me be a testimony to them also.

NOTES

THE BIBLE

Reading the Bible will open your mind.

Try reading the Bible, all the time.

The Bible will make you wise; it will make you believe,

but your blessings from the Lord you will receive.

The Bible is a very good book, and it will open your mind and heart.

By reading the good book, child the Lord, will do his part.

I read the Bible, and I do believe. It's a better to give, than to receive.

You'll find the knowledge, and wisdom too,

and I know God, is there for you

By James Green Jr.

More encouragement words from the author.

I pray also that you have been courage to never give up on yourself, or anyone, especially your immediate family. When you pray sincere prayers, the people that you are praying for may become bitter or angry. That is a sign that your prayers are working. I heard many testimonies where people asked someone to stop praying for them. The only reason that happens is because they are getting ready to receive a breakthrough and satan wants you to stop praying. They may come against you in any way. Remember, you are fighting battles in the spiritual ream. I advise you to keep your joy and peace. Don't stop praising God and thanking him for all he has done and all he is going to do. One day they will testify that I had a praying Father, Mom, Grandmother, Grandfather, Aunt, Uncle, Cousin, Wife, Husband, Sister, brother, or Friend that prayed for me. They took a little time and had me on their mind. It takes a lot of love to do anything that is good.

Sometimes things may look bad at the moment, but no one knows what that day or tomorrow may bring. It just like children, they may fight today and become friends the same day. Love should not bring about suffering, but happiness. Hurting people should not hurt others. There is a healing that needs to take place and ask God for help. God loves us all and will help us when we ask for it and stay humble. We must be thankful and grateful that we can have the victory in any situation. If we stand firm and do what we know is right and minister to others about the good things God has done for us.

Love,
Annie Lee

Printed in the United States
By Bookmasters